'Jean Gill's spiky humour makes you feel as if she's caught you on barbed wire and yet makes you smile about it' – Mike Sharpe, Haverfordwest Journalist

'...cuts clean through the icing with a cynic's knife. No scalpel delicacy here, but brutal slicing through the rich cake of life, exposing flaws as well as fruit – Jean Gill doesn't give a hoot! Often, a verse that starts with saccharine romance suddenly bursts out and kicks you in the pants.' – Derek Rees, The Guardian

'Jean Gill brings off the rare feat of looking life squarely in the eye without descending into dreary cynicism.' – H.S. Milford Haven Journalist

'...the humour frequently has the effect of pointing up the stark reality with which she writes.' – Ted Griffin, Pause Magazine

'An excellent collection – I enjoyed the sharpness and insight, the word-play... strong, fresh, vivid poems' – Robert Nisbet, author

'A delicious book full of the unexpected. Highly emotive contents.' – Writing Magazine

'Moving and varied' – Dorothy Tutin

Praise for *One Sixth of a Gill*, **Finalist in the Wishing Shelf Awards and the SpaSpa Awards for Literary Fiction**
'A superb collection... so much variation in style and all equally brilliant.' Karen Maitland, The Vanishing Witch

'A FINALIST and highly recommended... The author is particularly gifted with poetry.' The Wishing Shelf Awards

From Bedtime On

Jean Gill

2nd Edition © 2018 Jean Gill
The 13th Sign
All rights reserved.
ISBN 9791096459094
1st edition The National Poetry Foundation 1996

Cover design by Jessica Bell

Jean Gill's publications
Novels
The Troubadours Quartet
Book 4 Song Hereafter *(The 13th Sign)* 2017
Book 3 Plaint for Provence *(The 13th Sign)* 2015
Book 2 Bladesong *(The* 13th *Sign)* 2015
Book 1 Song at Dawn *(The 13th Sign)* 2015

Someone to Look Up To: a dog's search for love and understanding *(The 13th Sign)* 2016

Love Heals
Book 2 More Than One Kind *(The 13th Sign)* 2016
Book 1 No Bed of Roses *(The 13th Sign)* 2016

Looking for Normal (teen fiction/fact)
Book 2 Fortune Kookie *(The 13th Sign)* 2017
Book 1 Left Out *(The 13th Sign)* 2017

Non-fiction/Memoir/Travel
How Blue is my Valley *(The 13th Sign)* 2016
A Small Cheese in Provence *(The 13th Sign)* 2016
Faithful through Hard Times *(The 13th Sign)* 2017

Short Stories and Poetry
One Sixth of a Gill *(The 13th Sign)* 2014
From Bedtime On *(The 13th Sign)* 2018
With Double Blade *(The 13th Sign)* 2018

Contents

I Tamed Nine Tigers	*1, 41*
Creative Motherhood	*2, 41*
The Green Party	*3, 42*
Stored Treasure	*4, 42*
Where do you draw the line?	*5, 43*
Sensory Compensation	*6, 44*
Motorway Mausoleum	*8, 44*
Poem on the Underground	*9, 45*
Epilepsy: Fleurs du Mal	*10, 45*
Liberty's Department Store	*12, 47*
Party Pieces	*13, 47*
Sexist Generalisations	*14, 47*
Housewife: a feminine occupation	*15, 48*
Debating Final	*16, 48*
William's Herald	*18, 50*
Rupert of the Rhine	*19, 50*
And the rest was Pre-history	*20, 51*
Alternative Medicine	*21, 52*
No News is Good News	*22, 52*
A Teacher's Resignation	*23, 53*
And Grass Will Grow	*24, 53*
Alien Planet	*25, 54*
Biro Anthropology	*26, 54*
Deforestation	*27, 55*
Unwrapping Easter Eggs	*28, 55*
(Is There) Still Life	*29, 55*
Too Much of a Good Thing	*30, 56*
Eternity Ring	*31, 56*
A Fresh Start	*32, 57*
Dried Flowers and Dead Bees	*33, 57*
Lament of the Soldier's Lass	*34, 58*
Perfect Present	*35, 58*

Legacy	*36, 59*
Provence	*37, 59*
Hunting Trophies on the Loire	*38, 60*
One, Two, Three Little Words	*39, 61*
Jeanne d'Arc	*40, 61*

Section 2
The Stories Behind the Poems   *41*

Acknowledgements

Border decoration under Creative Commons License from www.webdesignhot.com

Cover artwork
Woman with bow: © lucky1984: Man in cup: © ivector

Poems published in Envoi, Iota, Orbis, Pause, Planet, Staple and Tandem

Special thanks to Johnathon Clifford, the National Poetry Foundation, for his mentoring, editing and personal encouragement

For Martin and Melissa

Introduction

This was my second collection of poetry, written during the late 1980s and early 1990s, when I was in my thirties, a fruitful time in both personal and professional life. *Not* in any order of priority: I was a mother; I married my second husband, John; and I gained promotion in my teaching career. I found new challenges in Gwendraeth Valley Comprehensive School, a rural comprehensive school in a naturally Welsh-speaking valley, known as 'the fly-half factory' because so many Wales rugby players in that position were ex-Gwendraeth boys.

By the time *From Bedtime On* was published, I was the newly appointed Headteacher of Graig Comprehensive School, a closing school that took 'challenge' to a new level. My claim to fame was in being one of the first two women to become a secondary Headteacher in Wales, sharing the honour and the irritations with Marina, who was appointed in Cardigan (a different county) at the same time.

Motherhood gave me new material and sharpened my writing. I experimented. Many of these poems are in highly structured verse forms. You'll find a sonnet, a villanelle and rhyming quatrains. I've also invented forms to suit the content. I'm always looking for that perfect marriage between form and content. The emotion comes in words, a shape, a rhythm.

As *The National Poetry Foundation* had published my first collection, I continued submitting work there. Slowly, my second book accumulated its contents: those poems deemed 'keepers'. My poems were published in top journals and I even won prize money from *Envoi*. Success at last!

The support and encouragement of my Editor, Johnathon Clifford, meant as much to me as did his creative editing, but he had strong preferences, and one poem that he rejected was chosen, years later, by Bloodaxe, for their anthology *Hallelujah for 50ft Women*. I have since learned not to write off my own work because of one negative opinion, whoever it comes from.

I was all set to collect poems for a third collection, when Johnathon broke the news to me that *The National Poetry Foundation* was only going to publish first collections from now on. I was on my own. I could have continued with new poetry, submitting work over and over to journals, entering competitions to win publication. Instead, I had a story that nagged at me, and, for the first time in my writing career, the form this story took was prose. Worse than that, it insisted on being a novel.

So, aged forty, at a high level in my career in education, I started writing my first novel, which did find a traditional publisher (Gomer) and was the first of many. I still write poetry and the selection in *One Sixth of a Gill* gained praise in *The Wishing Shelf Awards*.

When I give a poetry reading, I tell the stories behind the poems and so I thought it was time to add those to the written collection. I have kept the order of the poems as my Editor chose to print the first edition in 1996 but they are not in chronological order as written, so the stories behind them will be interwoven.

You'll find the stories behind the poems in a section at the back of the book. I hope they enrich the poems rather than explain them.

I TAMED NINE TIGERS

For you
I tamed nine tigers.
Mastery meant spearing meat
from buckets into drooling maws,
a pole's length from the flesh I fed them
to the meat I could become.

My spangled rump I turned
quite safely on the fenced-out crowd,
my eyes defying every yellow pair
which dropped in turn, defeated.
Bars on sawdust overshadowed
muscles shifting restlessly,
the camouflaged intent to kill
rippling under skins of sun on grass.

A snarl rebukes the missed beat
of my stare; fixed once more,
outbluffed by my belief
(I am more tiger,
deadlier by far than they)
a sullen tail swings threats,
then stills.

More tiger I
my voice a whip crack,
my pleasures purr and cuff
in play my anger death.

Nine tigers bowing
I present you.

CREATIVE MOTHERHOOD

Small patron of the arts, our son
commissioned songs at bed-time:
'Sing me the fork-lift truck.'
(A tricky one to rhyme and scan!)
'Our holiday to France... our dogs,'
replaced official nursery rhymes.
My poems died, no published work,
but on a summer's night I'd hear
the lilting saga of our life
in childish tones from bed-time on,
shaping his universe.

THE GREEN PARTY

Making someone small eat what he'd rather not
requires the sort of tactics that every mother's got
(or soon acquires). Supposing it's the veg
that makes for tea-time tantrums and a wedge
of strawberry-cake has lost its bribe appeal,
for your child to eat his greens the only answer
is to give a choice of meal.

Before you chop the veg up, in cook-to-adult tone,
ask 'Peas or beans? The choice is yours and yours alone.'
To be just like a grown-up with the right to choose between
makes him forget he hates all veg, not certain shades of green.
Choosing is confusing and cons him to believe
that what he gets is what he wanted not
what his mum let him receive.

Just like that cheated child, who eats his 'chosen' veg
I'm bribed, cajoled, bombasted by each politician's pledge.
This greener, better future which they say they offer me,
has horizons built of money on the dead dreams of the free.
Unless I stand for my beliefs myself, election means
that I'm doomed to cast my vote
for processed peas or processed beans.

STORED TREASURE

More gaps than teeth, face open to life,
unscarred, my son crawls on the carpet
in kneeless trousers, Turtles T shirt
and shoes beyond the scuff-coat care of polish.

His galleon sails to battle, manned with
pirates squeaking loud of war and
birthday parties – all their voices, his.

Since the 'Gulf Crisis', hostages and patriots
are mentioned often in the pirates' talk,
their strategies of war more detailed.

Less time is spent on parrot care
but even pirates hold their fire
to share some pop on treasure island,
declare a bedtime truce.

WHERE DO YOU DRAW THE LINE?

We used to 'draw the line' as kids;
a kind of 'chicken' game
between the sexes, one to one.
He'd put his finger-tip upon your nose
and trace a straight line
down your neck,
between your hope of breasts
and down... till you said,
'STOP!'
and did the same to him.

I always thought
'They went too far' meant
someone drew the line
courageous low.
We never reached below
the waist-band knicker line,
shamed by pictures in our minds
of what we touched and –
worse still – nearly reached.

Best players took their time;
some things don't change
no matter where you draw the line.

SENSORY COMPENSATION

Sighted people's touch can rarely pick out
braille, distinguish six-dot patterns.
Your fingers blur, distracted.

Decoding with your eyes is harder still,
a microscopic view of water-boatmen,
their dance mirage of pond.

And worse, one swimming insect's whole but
letters words are part- and slow collection
a t o m i s e s   s e n s e.

A student friend lost sight at seventeen,
learnt braille and used it for a year.
Her sight returned; her hands went blind.

However hard she shut her eyes
she felt as formless texture what had been
a favourite thought in classic text.

Reprieve was short. By diabetic lapse
she went stone-blind again. Why stone?
Glib qualifier of both blind and deaf

derived from feeling less than stone.
Feeling less.   Feeling loss,
expecting all the slow re-training (dog and self)

to cope with dangers in a visual world,
she found her fingers' sight returned on need.
Small miracle of compensation.

I would not give my eyes to tune pianos

but for one brightened night to read
the raised points of your skin with blind man's fingers
I might.

MOTORWAY MAUSOLEUM

That's a fine specimen (means dead).
A badger; never seen one living.
Victorians stuffed their wildlife
for glassy-eyed display in domes.
We passing glance at corpses
re-arranged on roads;
brief anatomy lesson
dividing men from beasts
by blankets only.
Humans go under cover. Dead.

POEM ON THE UNDERGROUND

Mind the gap! The tannoy nags us safely
up metal steps to strap-hang on the tube.
Mind the gap between the seats which may be
Perilously close and so intrude
Lewd touch on strangers, setting dangers free.
Don't let your baggage or cramped limbs protrude;
keep movements self-contained, a small grey flea
too insignificant to be considered rude:
Don't let your parcels nudge his foot or knee.
By no means sing, unless with headphones skewed
across your head to signal privacy;
nor unwrap, lick or swallow food.

Read poems on the wall to pass the time –
the inter-station gap's just fourteen lines
(I think I've found a form which suits it fine).

EPILEPSY: FLEURS DU MAL

Grand mal
Flower bursts of light draw down
to tunneled dark, a falling
sickness. À tes souhaits, à tes souhaits
we all fall down. A tissue
to wipe her mouth and forehead, gently.
So Sleeping Beauty blinked awake,
re-visiting a life she'd left, re-called,
recalling strange breath on her lips.

Perhaps that moment, after fitting,
before the contact breaks between
the real world and some other,
is momentary divinity –
the epileptic oracle.

Petit mal
The nervous system switches off,
takes forty winks of absence behind
the lightest gaze of eyes.
Then rapid blinks restore the power
of thought and hearing. Slightly dazed,
she's puzzled by the trickle
cooling down her leg.
They think she's strange;
sometimes she doesn't listen
and sometimes runs in shame
but won't say where or why.
The dandelions know,
les pissenlits

Nor-mal
The chemistry of body's finely balanced.

In love I overheat and stutter,
sob to choking when in grief.
Too many drinks and vision twists,
horizons heave to falling.
Allergic rashes bloom in clusters
through the spring and in response
to guinea-pigs or perfume.

We're rarely balanced,
rarely in control,
however we adjust our intake.
We're scared of cancer's roots
and analyse wild roses on our skin,
concoct our scientific posies
and need our friends to catch us
when we fall. We bless each other
holding hands; atishoo.

LIBERTY'S DEPARTMENT STORE

Between the glass and metal clones of chain stores,
revolving doors down-dated by carved oak,
Tudor black and white façade, five stories lit
with clothing brights and pale December faces.
Shoppers pushing, rushing, brushing past,
their bargains wielded high, broad shouldered
vanguard of the market forces.
A baby screams as angry knees and bags
collide and part at push-chair height.
His mother shushes, keeping a tight hold
on silky stockings (£5 off).

Once, this minstrel's gallery echoed
English song not dollars, marks or yen.
Now Arab robes command a feudal dip
from shop assistants beating a retreat
to rally by their banner at the tills
and serve the women masked in black,
ignoring those like me, 'just looking'.

PARTY PIECES

'It's difficult to tell
which women are related –
husbands' names you know.
I would have been impressed
if I had known she was *her* sister
not just *his* wife.
She should have told me when I asked
'And you are –?'
Instead she talked about her home
and woodland walks for God's sake.
I moved on sharpish
I can tell you. I mean
she should have said
about her sister –
Some people!'

Sometimes being outside suits,
but not tonight. It's like those dreams
but this time I am dressed while
every other's naked.
I watch and think but
there's no comfort in my observations –
envy rather than the freedom
to embarrass without pain,
without squirming for the self,
conscious.

We haven't met before.
Have you heard about my childhood,
my girlhood, my womanhood,
my hard-earned maturity?
Where have you gone?
Why doesn't anyone listen any more?

SEXIST GENERALISATIONS*

Man's talk is like
a team game where you intercept,
catch the topic and run with it,
assert yourself, avoid contact till
the interruption trips you up and
someone else is running while
you watch and catch your breath.
Listening helps you time your move.
You might even pass to team-mates
who'll get you straight back in the game.
It can be thrilling but not
when you're left speechless
on the sidelines.

Women like to agree,
to let ideas grow gently,
so that no-one knows
who said what first;
to make supportive contact,
through words of little meaning
but as strong as spider silk,
working nets of friendship.

Divergent thoughts will cross and bond,
tangential creation.
It's sociable and warm
provided no-one
flaunts her difference.

*based on reputable linguistic studies

HOUSEWIFE: A FEMININE OCCUPATION

She slashes the belly of a tube,
drips its last soap drops
into the plastic bowl
and scours the dishes
with abrasive pads;
whets the kitchen knife and
slices, dices, chops and carves
according to the density of flesh,
then seals the goodness in
with boiling water;
stuffs the metal drum
electrifies the circuits set
to pulverize the clothes clean
in chemical warfare
(enzymes versus germs);
gouges out the eyes
in red potatoes (best for baking).
Pillows pounded, cushions plumped,
she notes the time
and combs her hair.

She
kisses him and takes
her husband's coat.
Her welcome home is sweet
to him.
She's finishing her chores.

DEBATING FINAL

Te

You look to me for reassurance-
I cannot grade your guts. You speak
in hallowed halls lines with the privilege
you borrow for this hour's debate.
I teased you that you spoke to sheep
for practice (and in Welsh!)
yet we, without the money, shared
a breadth of vision not found here today.
I'm proud that you compete and shamed
the competition has not changed.
Who's top of which class in England?

Morituri

I'll die. The others speak so well,
my words dry into stutters and
all the careful wit falls flat.
They mince my arguments,
not with logic but contempt
for Welsh examples and an outside world.
'I rest my case, sure, ladies and gentlemen,
that...' a home crowd would have helped,

or drugs or being someone else!
Ruth, you're on. Miss Future Midwife,
please deliver us from evil.
Tell the one about the E.M.U.
getting off the ground. No, don't.
The laughter's not with us tonight.

Salutemus

You tried. Well done! You're here. Well done!
You died? Well done! No fear! Well done!

WILLIAM'S HERALD: 13th October 1066:

If you look close, you'll see me
sitting in the bows of William's ship
in all the usual colours – terracotta, buff and green
in crewels, laid-work on a linen background.
Saxon conscripts in an English workshop
paid this tribute to Bayeux and Bishop Odo –
there he is; so upright as he prays and praises
 righteous war. The Pope himself has blessed
the bloodshed Harold's broken oath has earned
and with his consecrated banner
sent St. Peter's hair as sacred token.
Other lads pass on my words, each to the next;
'Drop anchor; wait until you see light raised
on Mora's mast.' Too quick across,
uncertain landing holds our ships mid-sea.
My trumpet caught their ears and now
they call my message ship to ship.
I fancy as words travel our Duke William's
named the Bastard as at home
and named again from mouth to mouth
for what we hope – that William conquers.

RUPERT OF THE RHINE

Long black curls, a mournful droop of spaniel face,
lace-trimmed wrist arranged against green velvet,
the prince sits for the painter as still as
on the eve of Marston Moor, as finely costumed,
cavalier. Captured by his melancholy romance
I read his story, lived his battles,
could not understand how he died old
respected for his scientific finds,
not buckling swords or slashing ways.
Anachronistic knight, already odd
in days of arquebus and pike.
He speaks of noble codes in love and war.
How often have I mocked his kind,
sneering at their antique ways
when in this modern world they've tried
to speak, to touch my life with championed
lost cause and sacrificial gestures.
Romance is for dreamers; only in our dreams
do we respond, defences down.

AND THE REST WAS PRE-HISTORY

Dear Cro-Magnon Man,
    Many thanks for the flint.
It stands on the new Jurassic shelf,
just by the meadow-wort and flax
I cut and placed in sand. I think
I might try water next time.
Perhaps you'd like to join me for some food?
Broiled Mammoths chunks, I thought.
You'll like my latest paintings and
I've shaped some more words you could try.
(I know you find sounds difficult)
Please leave your club outside the cave,
I'm not that sort of mate.
Wo-man

ALTERNATIVE MEDECINE

Knot between eyes unravels as the pliant hands
glide over buttocks, breasts and thighs.
He touches pain they never tried to reach
with antiseptic gloves and tight-mouthed orders,
doubting almost that my pain was real,
my right to occupy their numbered bed.
'Relax; it hurts much less that way.
Hospital rules. We know what's best.'

Now, months later, brown hands chafe my skin
and slough off surface deadness, scouring circles.
Warm from Turkish baths, my body loosens,
makes the shape it's made to, bent to almost ache.
I thought that inmost pain had gone;
the whitecoats cut out what they could,
the rest I must have buried deep and dead.
What strangers sealed inside, this stranger healed,
kneading licensed warmth into a body
wrapped in layers to hide from cold regard.

I'd heard of Arab tourist traps, the men
whose little thrills you paid for, tourist game.
No-one told me of the healing hands
that rub and rinse the scum from polished limbs.
Wrapped in towels, I sip mint tea and glow and know
I'm free again to arc towards the sun.

NO NEWS IS GOOD NEWS

I cannot bear it but I watch the news
in hope of learning all I want to know,
So many people, such restricted views.

My children are so wearing to amuse,
I sometimes wish they'd hurry up and grow,
I cannot bear it but... I watch the news,

Though different countries' names at first confuse,
mass scenes of horror flash, repeat and go,
So many people, such restricted views.

If world events are really what they show,
whose world? Whose viewpoint? Not mine surely, so
I cannot bear it but I watch the news.

'Our person at the scene' provides the cues
for comments from the interviewed. They show
so many people, such restricted views.

The media angle always misconstrues
political awareness as a blow.
I cannot bear it but I watch the news;
so many people, such restricted views.

A TEACHER'S RESIGNATION

She'd said it many times before,
but no-one thought she'd meant it;
the times she'd slammed the staff-room door
and called the staff demented!

She'd said she'd have a little shop
and leave these brutes behind.
Like Tracy Gordon's Mum she'd give
one last piece of her mind.

No goodbyes; she'll leave us with
a scathing Yorkshire glance,
to strip the happy schooldays myth
to dirty underpants.

AND GRASS WILL GROW

Spring greens in the garden;
leaves unfurl, still wet and curling
from their winter buds. Sap rises,
underlies with subtle note
the hyacinth's brash drift.
past twitch of rabbit's nose
A snapped branch, soft footfall
causes bob, flick, scut, scoot.
Field is close enough to garden,
nudging with its weeds,
reminding us how quickly
grass will crack a tombstone, mock
our fashioning of wilderness.

ALIEN PLANET

Green politicians encourage
green supermarkets to sell
green products to green people.
Adverts used to play on envy's green;
we still buy what we're sold.
All those eco-safe 'necessities'
are packaged with our guilt
at ravaged landscapes.
What fourth world will we make
(as close to nature as the third
but with mod cons)?
Who's conned?
I pour more bleach into the sink;
it is the most effective whitener
for sepulchres.

BIRO ANTHROPOLOGY

Blood sacrifice still lurks beneath our smiles,
which threaten biting, contradicting words.
Blue blood of ink blots spread, a substitute
by which some expert judges mental state.
'Gaze into the blue-black pool and tell me
what you see,' (the witch doctor plays Rohrschach).
Pretend no recognition, but the shouted secrets form
subconscious shapes from chaos in 2D.
To word them, steal their power for his
vicarious thrill and private use, is this
the purpose after all of psychiatric skill?
I use a biro now, its vein controlled, contained;
no fountain welling up to spurt and flood,
no sign that people still write with their blood.

DEFORESTATION

Vigilance with tweezers, razors, fuzz-removers
keeps your hairy areas quite smooth
but cultivated plant life thrives on such attention,
spawning under-skin while you're asleep.

You envy those new tufted Europeans, guerillas
in a war dismissed in glossy magazines,
our choice made clear in photographs
of fashion models, air-brushed peachy smooth
perfection.

Wolves in disguise, we roam the high streets
clothing fears in jokes; first sign of madness?
Hairs on hand-backs. The second?
Looking for them...

UNWRAPPING EASTER EGGS

Ovulate for Easter,
emulate a broody hen;
let your body bring forth something
Risen Man can't claim for men.

Chocolate symbolism
of the stone rolled from the tomb
or cannibal adulation
of the eggs inside your womb?

(IS THERE) STILL LIFE

Containers fascinate,
conceal their contents though
their purpose is so plain.

Metal shines like water;
too smooth for pewter,
too ornate for stainless steel,
the tea pot sits, an object.

Its mate, artistically behind
and slightly to the left,
shows purity of line
in duller stone, a pitcher.

Connection's indirect; they pour
their hearts out, never touch.

TOO MUCH OF A GOOD THING

If you followed every smile
to its natural conclusion,
to sagas of love, friendship,
tears, laughter, death;
strangers would seem deadlier
than if mere violence lurked
beneath their smiles. Closeness
strains. Imagine then if
cumulative links for life
were forged from *every* contact,
no opportunity missed...
be grateful you can just smile
back and go.

ETERNITY RING

Looking back, she told him of the ways
she'd fallen short before,
the faults and failings starkly drawn –
as they had been to her.

He told her there were those who'd fault
a diamond for not being glass.
She turns his word to catch the light,
her flaws made facets of their love.

A FRESH START

Something in me will not start again
with pleasure at each mug, each lamp-shade,
every careful choice of colour for the home.

I choose (again) a hoover, then sit on a step.
I made the big choice, isn't that enough,
without this memory-mocking game?

So leave the shopping, take me to our room
which smells of damp and resignation.
Make me tea and stroke my feet, then catch

my thoughts before they've left me.
If nothing else, at least we've learnt
what doesn't make a home

DRIED FLOWERS AND DEAD BEES

Someone once told me –
perhaps it is true –
that a bee's first-found flower
is its only. This view

is romantic; it means
if the lavender's faded
the bee will do too,
who seeks only lavender,
lavender rue.

I feel for the bee
at the fade of its flower.
We hunger for true love but
fear its last hour.

LAMENT OF THE SOLDIER'S LASS

Just like he'd go and get the coal
or put the dustbins out;
my love would kill in army drill
for his manhood downs his doubt.

Yes, downs his doubt in one, they'd say
and takes it like a man
while I would cry and wonder why
I can't do what he can.

PERFECT PRESENT

My present wrenched from
brown paper and string,
you paused and asked,
'Why so plain a wrapper?'

'Look around,' I answered,
'at the white-washed walls
and bare wood floorboards, the setting
where we live and wish.
If rainbows are for touching
they should come plain cover, to protect us
from the spite of jealous gods.
I give you this rainbow;
a child would wish for further wishes,
we know that magic dies with use –
what do you wish?'

A pause, then
irritation clouds your eyes.
'I wish... you would not buy me
such expensive presents –
we can't afford to pay for this.'

LEGACY

Her head full of visions, Berthe Morisot painted
Parisian cafés, girls swirling in smiles;
impressions of colour kaleidoscope round.
Dreaming academies, galleries, fame, she paused,
distracted by a little tugging hand.
'Maman, for me please?' She sighed,
dipped paint brush, faltered, then
firmly added 'A' in stylish strokes
on top of figures, landscaped thoughts,
'B', 'C' to 'Z', the childish labels
desecrated canvas, declaring to the future
an artist's love, a mother's art.
A young girl sleeps, her head full of visions
Berthe Morisot painted.

PROVENCE

Where blue and yellow are not names
but shouts of power to call an artist home,
a sun-baked lizard on pink stone
is startled into animation –
gone from one frame to the next;
the picture flickers.
Plane trees peeled like ageing paint,
festive with fairy lights,
spread shade in market squares
more subtle than Martini parasols.
Olives daub their blue-grey haze
of leaf clouds over knuckled bark.

Poplars, deep, most formal green
point threats, invite the thunder.
Stunted oaks, wing sculpted,
stagger down the slopes where
bergamot, crushed thyme and sweat
beat down before the thunder breaks.

HUNTING TROPHIES ON THE LOIRE

Tourists play peek-a-boo at facing windows,
part up spiral stairs; Chambord's double helix
petrifies our genes in grandeur,
creamy stone with flecks of prince's gold.
Did kings play peek-a-boo in this,
their hunting lodge? Stand below
the boar's head, bums against the fire?
Children's fretful shouts and echoes
from the multi-lingual tourist guides
jog my camera arm to action.
I came here as it's on my list
of places I should visit; I shoot
another trophy for my wall.

ONE, TWO, THREE LITTLE WORDS

One little word
was the beginning
allegedly.

Supporting evidence exists;
their words weighted with
evolutionary millennia
parents say
'Stop creating!'
'Just one word and...'

You gave me two words
needed for my poem.
I tried to pay you back but
you didn't like the words
I chose. Sorry,
I should have said
'Thank you.'

Olympic medal won
the lean-shanked long-distance runner
turns towards the international cameras
and writes i l y in the air
across the airwaves to his wife
who can't be there but shares his moment
privately publicly.

JEANNE D'ARC

Short-haired in peasant browns
with coarse hands clasped in prayer,
another virgin fed to dragons,
bound maidenly in place.

Eyes aflame, her fakir's trance
wafts angels over faggots;
clothes shrivel to autumnal leaves
scatter ashes, shrive the madness
sparked by nations of the time.

'Follow me!' she cried, 'For France!'
and stirred a nation's stolid soldiers,
'Mon Dieu,' as always
coupled with 'Mon Droit!'

Man-like. Burned for that?
Or dangerous, if womanly?
She led so many men and
answered all the questions wrong.

Like science, Inquisition-banned
and martyred by the rules she broke.
Difficult company, my name-saint
(and all those visions to consult).

It is not safe to let the others know
you see what they do not.

.

The Stories Behind the Poems

I Tamed Nine Tigers

One of my ambitions as a little girl was to be a tiger-tamer in a circus and, as an adult, I did watch a woman controlling nine tigers in the ring, with her whip and rewards of meat. Nowadays, I can't switch off my awareness of animal welfare concerns but at the time I was fascinated. Part of me still feels disappointed that I never tested myself with these beautiful, dangerous beasts, and they became a metaphor for all the wild urges I have controlled, from love. This poem was a gift to my husband, John, for whom I tamed nine tigers that were more dangerous than he will ever realise.

Creative Motherhood

There are several autobiographical poems in this collection on the theme of motherhood and love for a child. I *loved* being a mother but didn't see why I should fit into anybody else's notion of what that meant. I was very happy continuing in my work as a teacher and, although life was crazy-busy, I think it was less stressful for me than if I'd tried to be a stay-at-home mother. I've always believed that a martyr-mother makes for a bad role model so I don't go in for sacrifices – too much blood, to quote Roger McGough. How on earth do you know what's best for your child, long-term? If in doubt, do what's best for you (and your long-suffering partner) and share the fulfillment with your child, is what works for me. I was lucky to have such a supportive husband, who never saw parenting as *my* job.

It's true that I stopped writing while my son was very young, which could have been frustrating, but it wasn't. I think 'creativity' can be expressed in many ways, including motherhood. I did indeed make up songs for him, to order, and he *was* very partial to fork-lift trucks. As in any oral tradition, there is no record of those songs, but they were fun, and tricky to create. To light the creative spark in another human being is as fulfilling as putting words on a page; that's also how I feel about my best work as a teacher, with children or adults. When I heard my little boy singing the story of his life, as he lay in bed, I felt fulfilled, creatively.

The Green Party

This is my political poem and it still holds true! I was using that well-known parental tactic of conning a child into eating vegetables by offering a choice (of vegetable), at the same time as listening to an election campaign, when I had my lightbulb moment. We had a choice between peas and beans. The party leaders had more in common with each other, as did their policies, than with me and my political views. Appropriately the Green Party had just been formed in the U.K. (in 1990) so that gave me the perfect title.

Stored Treasure

My son used to crawl around the carpet, playing with his lego pirate ship, holding the pirates as they talked to each other. He used different squeaky pirate voices for the different characters. The Gulf War was on the news (1991) and suddenly the pirates were talking about hostages and weapons (patriots), interspersed with the usual tea-parties. I was surprised at how many cups of tea and how much cake pirates ate, but saddened at the effect of war on a small child's vocabulary. Of course, he was lucky to know war only on television but I did wonder what messages reach children from 'the world'. Doesn't every mother want to protect her child and don't we also know how impossible it is? I can't untangle 'cute' from 'sad' in the observation that led to this poem.

The Teenage Mutant Ninja Turtles were a very popular cartoon at the time, hence the T-shirt, and it's refreshing to think how many children from that era know of Donatello, Raphael, Leonardo and Michelangelo. Contact with 'the world' is not all bad.

Where do you draw the line?

We played this VERY naughty children's game when I was eleven, in 1966, in Cockton Hill Junior School, Bishop Auckland. I looked up the school site and nowadays it apparently offers 'an exciting and engaging school curriculum'. As a soldier's daughter, I moved schools frequently, and spent only six months in this one, which was fairly wild. I was bullied for my accent, for being a snob, for having a tartan briefcase... No doubt it all made me strong.

Another wild game that we played in the yard was 'tag and faint'. I have no idea how the psychology worked but one kid would draw a spiral inwards on another kid's back and 'pull the string' at which point the more sensitive volunteers would faint. I never fainted so was no fun. I wrote this game into my teen novel *Fortune Kookie* along with my later experiments in Ouija board and vaguely supernatural games, with the same gang. I would have been scared if I thought my own children had got up to some of the things we did!

Sensory Compensation

One of my friends at university was blind and this is partly her story, partly love poem (for John, as always). My friend lost her sight at sixteen, through diabetes, and learned braille. I am fascinated by the ability to read braille as I just can't feel the bumps with enough sensitivity, even if I shut my eyes. I wanted to describe my experience of trying to read braille in the sighted equivalent, which is why I spaced out the letters on one line.

My friend told me that when she briefly regained her sight, she couldn't read braille any more, which made me think about sensory compensation: the notion that when you lose (or are born without) one sense, the other senses compensate. Braille requires super-sensitive touch. Tuning pianos requires perfect pitch and the man who tuned our school piano was blind. My train of thought led me to wonder what it would be like to have no sight but my other senses heightened. Imagine making love.

Motorway Mausoleum

I still haven't seen a living badger although one of my Welsh friends has them regularly raiding her dustbin. I remember visiting York Natural History Museum and being horrified by the Victorian stuffed animal collection, and by the whole idea that somebody interested in animals would capture them and kill them for display 'in the interests of science'. And yet I didn't react with the same awareness of human responsibility for road-kill. Each society has its own blind spots, while feeling superior to others.

Poem On The Underground

During a coffee-break at a festival, one of the other writers told me that the gap between tube stations (subway or metro stations in non-British English) is exactly fourteen lines of poetry. This is a very silly idea but it tickled my fancy.

Fourteen lines suggested a sonnet to me so I used the Shakespearian sonnet form (three stanzas rhyming abab and then a rhyming couplet cc). I made it more difficult by only using two rhymes through the four quatrains (four-line stanzas) but I made it easier by using half-rhyme (time/lines/fine). The underlying meter (rhythm and syllables) is the traditional iambic pentameter (ten syllables to a line and boo-boom boo-boom stressed to make the rhythm).

Then I added one more line to make it the only fifteen-line sonnet so you miss your tube stop. Technically, this is the most fun I've ever had without a poetic form and the content comes from several journeys around London, being told to 'Mind the gap'. Now you know; the important gap is fourteen lines.

Epilepsy: Fleurs du Mal

Two of my students were epileptic and I learned to recognize the signs in one girl of what was sometimes called *'petit mal'*, 'the little illness', when somebody briefly loses consciousness without it being noticeable to those not looking for the signs. She would look absent and be confused when conscious again. One problem of *'petit mal'* is losing bladder control. The other student suffered full epileptic seizures, and could fall down and froth at the mouth if her medication was not keeping a balance.

I used these facts in the poem along with some historical beliefs about epilepsy. Caesar was supposedly epileptic, and a seizure was taken to be a sign of genius, or of divine possession.

Then I mixed in the traditional children's rhyme and some allusions to Baudelaire (the French poet, whose work left music and quotations in my imagination). *Ring-a-ring of roses* has the chorus *'We all fall down'* so that seemed appropriate and *'Atishoo, atishoo'* came from the French *'A tes souhaits,'* 'Bless you,' so it all seemed to work with the French term *'petit mal'*.

Baudelaire's great work was *Les Fleurs du Mal*, *The Flowers of Evil*, so with *'grand mal'* and *'petit mal'* as terms for epilepsy, and the flowers of *'ring-a-ring of roses'*, I found patterns and connections. *'Pissenlits'* the French word for dandelions, literally means 'Piss-a-bed', a term for the flower also used in medieval English.

I have always thought about what 'normal' might mean and the play on the French *'mal'*, in *Nor-mal*, signalled my vision of how my experiences are like those of my two students. Haven't we all lost control sometimes and needed help?

Liberty's Department Store, London

On my occasional visits to London, I loved going into Liberty's. It's a spectacular half-timbered medieval building with old oak paneling and minstrel galleries inside. When I wrote the poem, in the 1990s, I had done well enough in my career to afford a suit there in the sale. I remember the soft feel of the herring-bone tweed, and the cut of the jacket. Many of the customers were Arabs and, in those days, were more likely to be rich foreign tourists than locals. I imagined these customers as the new aristocrats in what I thought was a centuries-old building. Thanks to the Internet, I now know this is a mock-Tudor building built in 1924. Perhaps that makes it even more remarkable.

Party Pieces

I see parties or social gatherings as work and I dislike the kind of loud English person who wants to meet important people and for whom you are categorized by your relationship with an important person (if you have one). The second voice is a version of me, with a self-critical awareness that such a woman is not the ideal party companion.

Sexist Generalisations

One of the many courses I attended as a teacher looked at students' preferred learning styles and gender differences. The tendency was for men to compete, and for women to keep their heads down and play as a team. Apart from the fact that individuals might not fit the boxes, what struck me is that you can suffer from not fitting in, whichever the talk style. Understanding what I was 'doing wrong' didn't change my behaviour much but at least I knew why I didn't meet women's expectations or expectations of women.

Housewife: a feminine occupation

Irony is fun and the word 'feminine' just begs to be mocked. I used to consider 'housewife' to be an insult, usually preceded by the word 'little'. My mother was a 'housewife' and worked very hard so I knew what the job entailed. That's what amused me: the fact that 'housewife' was a job, and that 'keeping your man' went with the 'wife' part of the job. Domestic chores give a wonderful opportunity for controlled violence and that old-fashioned moment when the housewife takes off her apron and prepares for the man's homecoming always seemed open to the interpretation I've given in the poem: she's finishing her chores.

Debating Final

The structure of the poem uses the Latin phrase uttered by gladiators as they went into the arena to tear each other apart or to face wild beasts: *'Te morituri salutemus',* 'We who are about to die salute you.' The gladiators were two girls in Gwendraeth Valley Comprehensive School debating team, which I helped coach, and the arena was a very posh private school in London where the competition final was held. It was amazing that students from a Welsh valley comprehensive school should reach the final and the girls were sharp and witty. This competition required interaction between two competing teams, along the lines of the House of Commons' Question Time, not just prepared speeches. However much the girls prepared, they could not compete with their own nerves, faced with the English accents and social poise that come from private education.

I was incredibly proud of them, for their courage in being there, for their performance, however nervous, but the social class system hit me during our visit. We weren't used to so many courses at a meal, each with its own different alcohol, finishing with port. The hospitality felt as intimidating as the 'hallowed halls' in which the debate took place.

Our idea of politics was far more liberal, more international than was that of the competition and it was difficult for the girls to deliver their jokes in such an atmosphere of privilege. Wales is indeed a different country but many British politicians *have* grown up there; not many women politicians in the 1990s though.

The teacher (me) speaks in the first and last stanza. Ruth, one of the team, did indeed want to be a midwife and her team-mate was Eirian. The E.M.U. was the European Monetary Union, in the days when the euro was but a dream. And the emu not getting off the ground was Ruth's favourite joke, which went down well in Wales. Nowadays we'd make euro jokes or – how wicked! – make fun of sterling.

The girls were disappointed. They didn't give their best performance but things would have been different in a home match! I wrote the poem because I wanted the girls to know how proud I was of them. Proud enough to put it in writing.

William's Herald

This poem won enough prize money to pay for half the costs of the weekend we spent in Bayeux, which inspired the poem. The Bayeux Tapestry and the history behind it was even more interesting than I'd thought it would be, and I was drawn to the characters of the lads, with horns, passing messages between the ships. I'd read some poems by Sheenagh Pugh, written in the first person as historical characters, and I imagined what William's herald might be shouting (and thinking) as the ships sailed across the Channel for that historic battle. Those pivotal moments in history make a for a good story and fun with hindsight. At this point, William was known as 'the Bastard' and the herald speculates that his new nickname could be based on what they all hope 'that William conquers'.

One fact that really surprised me was that the tapestry was made in England, by Saxons, probably commissioned by William's half-brother, Bishop Odo, who joined in the condemnation of the oath-breaker Harold and called down God's vengeance against him. Imagine how those Saxon women (most likely) must have felt sewing the story of their defeat! Yet they produced a masterwork. Maybe *that* is the real winner. There is certainly a story to be told about the makers of the tapestry.

Rupert of the Rhine

As a young teenager, I read historical novels and fell in love with Rupert of the Rhine. I even had a pencil drawing of him inside my wardrobe, copied from a portrait I found in the library. With his long black curls and cavalier background, he was the perfect historical rock star. What teenage girl ever fell in love with a roundhead? Margaret Irwin's novel *The Stranger Prince* added a doomed love affair to Rupert's military defeat at Marston Moor with his legendary poodle, Boy, always with him in battle. It does seem strange that such a romantic figure returned with Charles II, became known as a scientist and died at sixty-three – my age, as I write this, so it doesn't seem old any more! Stranger still to find him described online as a 'German soldier', he who epitomized the dashing English cavalier, when I was growing up. When I wrote this poem, I owned up to my romantic streak. I still have a soft spot for Rupert of the Rhine, and my troubadour hero Dragonetz los Pros displays some of Rupert's talents: military, engineering and, of course, romantic.

And the rest was Pre-history

We had a holiday in Dorset with extended family. My brother-in-law found a fossil and presented it to me, and I had a sudden image of a caveman offering a similar present to a woman. I played with the idea of a man being 'Neanderthal', with gender stereotypes and with so many discoveries yet to come, such as keeping flowers alive by placing them in water. In my version of pre-history, the woman creates cave-paintings and makes discoveries. Historians so often write their own prejudices into theories about the past, and I've always been annoyed when told that cave artists must have been men, so the role reversal reflects a serious challenge to received views. However, the poem is a light-hearted representation of male-female roles and is looking for a smile in response, not a demo. The woman is also fussy and house-proud (not like me!).

Alternative Medicine

Years after the experience, I wrote this poem about a massage I was given in Tunis by an Arab masseur. Nowadays, massages are more common, but this was the only professional massage in the first forty years of my life, and it affected me deeply. I went to Tunisia while still in shock from my second miscarriage and from bad hospital experiences with 'whitecoats'. The Turkish bath, polish and massage, had an intimacy that was opposite in impact to what I'd suffered. I felt shy at allowing a stranger's touch on my naked torso but, afterwards, I felt that something had been healed. My French physiotherapist sometimes says, *'Nous avons liberé quelque chose,'* and that's what healing hands do: they 'liberate something.'

No News is Good News

The title is an ironic play on the old saying, turning it on its head to mean 'There is only bad news,' and I did indeed grow angry when I watched the TV news. This is very much my point of view being expressed, although I took the liberty of making 'children' plural because it scanned better than my actual, one, young child. Apart from raging at the stories themselves, I was angry at the absence of women. An alien would have had the impression that women were 5% of the population to judge by their presence or mention on 'the news'. I think the strict poetic form I used (a villanelle) kept that anger under control so that, instead of my usual rant on the subject, the message is calm. This is definitely a poem with a message, but I think it allows readers to respond with their own thoughts. The villanelle form requires that whole lines are repeated, in an alternating pattern and I think that is enough to strengthen the message, without me shouting. The disadvantage of a villanelle is that the repetition can be boring so the repeated lines have to be strong enough to bear repetition. My favourite villanelle ever is Wendy Cope's *Reading Scheme* where she limits herself to the vocabulary of a *Peter and Jane* Ladybird reader for children, to convey an adult message.

A Teacher's Resignation

What goes on in school staff-rooms would make a book in itself! After being treated badly by students, one of my colleagues, a French teacher, burst through the door that separated the pupils from our sanctuary and, having safely closed said door, launched into a tirade that was pretty much word-for-word what I shaped into a rhyming poem. I like using rhyme for poems that bite, that are *not* sweet, as I think there is an irony in that clash of expectations. Rhyme is associated with greeting cards, children's songs and love poems, so I like spicing it up. I'm by no means the only one to do so, and I have enormous respect for the wry rhymes of Pam Ayres and Victoria Wood. Most teachers make a speech like this at some time in our careers. Then the bell goes and we patrol the mean streets once more, superheroes in disguise.

And Grass Will Grow

This is my *Ozymandias* poem. Shelley wrote, '*Look on my Works, ye Mighty, and despair!*' only to show the decay wrought by desert sands on what was supposed to be immortal architecture. In the same way, in my poem, wilderness will always reclaim a garden and grass will crack a tombstone. I like the idea that nature is immortal and human works temporary. I hope this proves to be true and that life itself is stronger on this planet than human impact on the environment, but I am less optimistic than I used to be when I was twenty and a conservation volunteer. I do have my own little piece of wilderness here in Provence: an orchard visited by deer, wild boar and hare, and where the workers from my beehive *Endeavour* busy themselves. Keeping bees is my way of doing something, however small, for this planet I have loved so much.

Alien Planet

The title plays on the ideas that we should all be 'green' and that aliens are 'little green men'. Written in the 1990s, this poem still expresses some of my observations and questions on 'green issues'. The combination of guilt and hypocrisy that we carry has grown heavier, not lighter. We are still conned by 'mod cons' that we don't need and by advertising that plays on 'green issues' to *sell* us things we don't need. If my sixteen-year-old eco-warrior self could see today's society, she would be overjoyed at all the recycling and horrified at all the ridiculous, unnecessary packaging.

Biro Anthropology

I'd need a psychologist (or a witch-doctor) to analyse the state of mind that produced *this* poem! I've always been fascinated by the Rorschach test, in which subjects express what they see in an ink blot. I've used inkblots in workshops to stimulate creative writing and I found the results revealing – as were responses to photos of doors, or plates of cake. You can psycho-analyse any creative output to any stimuli but I'm not convinced that the result is scientific. However, the link

I've made between pools of ink and pools of blood, between smiling and aggressively baring teeth – that's all a bit deep! Luckily I've never had the pleasure of being psycho-analysed so I leave that to my readers.

Deforestation

We British women all know that body hair is the enemy, and that we will grow whiskers and turn into cats as we age – or into werewolves. European women used to be known for having non-shaved underarms and legs but fashions in body hair come and go. The joke in the last lines was popular in my junior school, when I was about eleven, and seemed apt.

Unwrapping Easter Eggs

Part of losing my religion was becoming aware of patriarchal versus matriarchal symbolism, and of the way Christian celebrations incorporated older, pagan traditions. This is a wickedly irreverent poem, pointing out the female symbolism of eggs at the heart of the most sacred festival in the Christian Year.

(Is There) Still Life

I was invited along to a meeting of Swansea Writers' Group in Wales, to give a poetry workshop and I took my collection of pictures and photos, which I sometimes use as a stimulus. On this occasion, everybody chose one image and said something about it. Then I gave further prompts, until everyone had written some lines. Then we shaped our lines into a first draft of a poem. I joined in. The picture I chose was a painting of a jug and a teapot, a still life, just as I describe in the poem. While writing I realised all the meanings in the artist's term 'still life' and how separate each of those two objects was from the other. We finished the session by reading our poems aloud and I stuffed mine into my file. I took it out later, decided I still liked it, worked on it some more and it was published in *Pause*, then accepted for this, my second book of poetry with *The National Poetry Foundation*. The editor's method was to read and review six poems at a time from me, marking those accepted for the book and writing his criticisms on those rejected. Tough love but I learned from it.

Too Much of a Good Thing

Think of all those missed opportunities, when an attractive person smiled an invitation at you, and you didn't follow up. What if you had followed up on every possible relationship, developing it to its full potential? Exactly. Overwhelming! What a nightmare! The idea came from Hermann Hesse's novel *Steppenwolf*, which was one of my favourite books. The main character can enter doors in a magical corridor, which take him back to those 'missed encounters' and allow him to live all those experiences. Despite my pragmatic poem, I still find the idea attractive.

Eternity Ring

This is another of those poems where I write about myself in the third person. It's based on a few precious words spoken by John when we were first together, when I told him all the many things that were wrong with me. His image of diamonds and glass was the most beautiful compliment in my life, and, like an eternity ring, was a promise of being together forever. I do have over-romantic expectations of life (one of the faults listed) so it's very gratifying when life exceeds them.

A Fresh Start

It is not easy to start again in a second (or third) marriage, after divorce. This poem is also autobiographical. Sometimes it was the little things, such as buying a hoover (vacuum-cleaner), that brought back memories of first-time-round, of being a first-time newly-wed, with pleasure in all those purchases for a first home. You carry those memories with you, and they can cause hurt, and be a barrier to a fresh start. But if the relationship is strong enough, you also know what doesn't make a home and you don't make the same mistakes.

Dried Flowers and Dead Bees

We spent several camping holidays in Provence and I liked visiting the *Musée d'Abeille* (Bee Museum) in Riez, under the pretext that it was educational for my son. Each time, I grilled the beekeeper in bad French about his passion, and one of the snippets of information he passed on was that a bee would seek out only the flower she first found.

True or not, this love affair between a bee and one type of flower stayed in my imagination, and turned into this little poem. Who'd have thought that, years later, I would train in Provence as a beekeeper? There is still so much we don't know about bees. Each winter I worry whether my bees will survive till spring and each April (so far) I heave a huge sigh of relief. I am still fascinated by bees. I can also testify that your own honey, produced from your own land, by the bees you've cared for, tastes better than any other honey in the world.

Lament of the Soldier's Lass

This was intended as a modern take on the old ballads the days of the *Johnnie-went-a-soldiering type*. Although it has dated because, nowadays, women *are* combat soldiers, the notion that separating gender rôles has pros and cons is still valid. I think of WW2 and the men being called up to go to war. Although I have argued hard for equal rights, I am not filled with joy at the thought that I, a woman, could be called up to fight in WW3.

Perfect Present

There are many ideas wrapped up in the brown paper and string of this poem. Mindfulness and appreciating the moment, the 'present'; values that have nothing to do with money, or how much a gift cost; a human relationship of shared values. One irony in the last lines is the twist on a gift being 'too expensive'. There is friction between a couple over gifts above their income but here, the gift is free and yet priceless; a wish. As in all the parables of old, the recipient wastes the wish in a spiteful, trivial jibe. At the heart of any gift is the relationship and here, a beautiful offering is misunderstood and rejected.

The January sunsets have been spectacular here in Provence this year, and we have been calling each other to look: *'Have you seen the clouds over there?'* I've been reminded of this poem and of gifts that should be treasured.

Legacy

I feel cheated each time I come across a woman who was famous in her day, talented and successful – and whose name disappeared from the history I was taught in school. Why did I not know about all these amazing women?! One such was the Impressionist painter Berthe Morisot and when I was reading about her work, I came across the fact that she defaced some of her paintings to make an ABC primer for her child's enjoyment. I'm partly horrified (works of art vandalized!) and partly exhilarated (a mother's joy in sharing her art with her child). What could be more creative than sharing your work with another human being and shaping his/her own creativity? Although I'm no Berthe Morisot this is the same train of thought as in my poem *Creative Motherhood*. Both motherhood and teaching can be intensely creative and, instead of a product like a book or a painting, there are moments of joy and connection.

Provence

John promised me that he would take me to the south of France and, when he kept his word, I fell in love with the light and the landscape. When I was prompted to write about a landscape, Provence came first to mind, even though the workshop was in Llandovery on a grey Welsh day. The writer leading my group of students was Paul Hyland, whose poetry is as good as the travel books he is known for. I sat in a corner and wrote my own poem quietly, while he encouraged and motivated the students to write their pieces with a sense of place. We were so lucky in Wales to have writers of such quality coming into our schools, weaving magic with youngsters of all abilities. What Gillian Clarke started and championed, others continued, and I have worked as both writer and teacher in such events.

It is good for teachers to be once more the students: under pressure to write well, worried you won't, afraid to look foolish in public and then, with an experienced leader, surprised that you've written something you like, that you are willing to share – something you can take home with you.

Hunting Trophies on the Loire

Chambord is one of those famous, overwhelming Loire chateaux, whose every architectural feature is meant to impress. You can just wander round saying, 'Wow!' as was intended, or you can imagine real people trying to stop saying, 'Wow!' and to get on with real lives in such surroundings. I love fireplaces and my experience of open fires is that when people walk into a room, they stand in front of the fire, warming their bums, so that's how I tried to make Chambord real to me. Men in powdered wigs, breeches and clocked stockings, bums to the fire. As it was supposedly a shooting lodge, the play on the word 'shoot' amused me as all the tourists wandered round with our cameras.

One, Two Three Little Words

The title came from the popular TV game, a form of charades, and the poem started with the long-distance runner winning a gold medal in the 1980 Moscow Olympics. John told me that, in his moment of triumph, Steve Ovett mimed i l y for the TV camera, a message to his wife, many miles away. A private message in a public place had personal meaning for me too, between the two of us, and the story resonated. Those were the three little words.

One word was an easy jump of thought for anybody brought up on bible readings: *'In the beginning was the word'*. I had fun with the double meaning of 'create' as I often heard it used of naughty children: they were 'creating'.

'Two words' came from one of those spiky moments, where you've said the wrong thing, upset the other person without knowing why, and 'Thank you' was what you should have said.

Jeanne d'Arc

If I were French, my name would be Jeanne and Jeanne d'Arques (Joan of Arc) would have been my patron saint. Instead of my birthday, I would celebrate her fête. Add to this the fact that she had visions, led armies, advised a king and dressed as a man, and you can understand why this medieval heroine captured my interest. There are many different theories as to *why* she was condemned by the Inquisition and burned at the stake; politics and expediency seem as likely as the heresy that formed an excuse. Whether visions were heresy or miracle was after all a matter for Church judgement. Dressing up as a man and winning battles might have been more of a sticking point. As I always conclude, being different does not go down well. But at least nobody's threatened me with the stake yet.

If you liked my book, please help other readers find it by writing a review.

Thank you.

For exclusive offers and news of my books,
and a FREE ebook of
One Sixth of a Gill,
please visit jeangill.com and sign up for my newsletter.
This collection of shorts and poems was a finalist in
the Wishing Shelf and *SpaSpa Awards*.

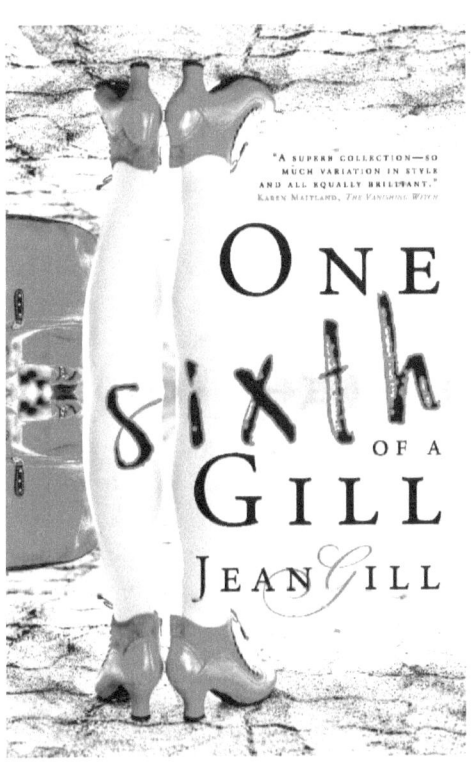

About the Author

I'm a Welsh writer and photographer living in the south of France with two scruffy dogs, a beehive named *Endeavour*, a Nikon D750 and a man. I taught English in Wales for many years and my claim to fame is that I was the first woman to be a secondary headteacher in Carmarthenshire. I'm mother or stepmother to five children so life has been pretty hectic.

I've published all kinds of books, both with conventional publishers and self-published. You'll find everything under my name from prize-winning poetry and novels, military history, translated books on dog training, to a cookery book on goat cheese. My work with top dog-trainer Michel Hasbrouck has taken me deep into the world of dogs with problems, and inspired one of my novels.

With Scottish parents, an English birthplace and French residence, I can support the winning team on most sporting occasions.

Someone To Look Up To

For all dog-lovers!
Someone to Look Up To. A dog's life in the south of France based on true stories from Jean Gill's work with top international dog trainer, Michel Hasbrouck.

From puppyhood, Sirius the Pyrenean Mountain Dog has been trying to understand his humans and train them with kindness...

How this led to divorce he has no idea. More misunderstandings take Sirius to Death Row in an animal shelter, as a so-called dangerous dog learning survival tricks from the other inmates. During the twilight barking, he is shocked to hear his brother's voice but the bitter-sweet reunion is short-lived. Doggedly, Sirius keeps the faith.
One day, his human will come.

Jean Gill's award-winning series
The Troubadours Quartet
History was never more exciting!

1150 in Provence

'Historical Fiction at its best.' Karen Charlton, *the Detective Lavender Mysteries*

Set in the period following the Second Crusade, Jean Gill's spellbinding romantic thrillers evoke medieval France with breathtaking accuracy. The characters leap off the page and include amazing women like Eleanor of Aquitaine and Ermengarda of Narbonne, who shaped history in battles and in bedchambers.

www.ingramcontent.com/pod-product-compliance
Lightning Source LLC
LaVergne TN
LVHW092057060526
838201LV00047B/1437